In Case of an Emergency

Young Voices

Edited by Josie Moon and Nick Triplow

A **La Luna** Publication 2017

Published by La Luna Books 2017
152 Rutland Street
Grimsby
DN32 7NE

www.josiemoon.co.uk

ISBN 978-0-9957284-2-4

Cover design and illustrations: Sophie Helen Ashton
Layout by Paul Davy www.davyart.co.uk
Printed by GSB Print & Design | 30 Hainton Avenue | Grimsby
| North East Lincolnshire | DN32 9BB | T. 01472 287362

Contents

FOREWORD

This sparkling first collection of poetry, prose and image from Franklin Young Voices showcases a breadth of imagination and talent. These are distinct 21st century voices on life, love and everything in between.

Special thanks to Josie Moon at La Luna Press for her vision and making this dream a reality and Nick Triplow for sharing his support expert guidance.

Carolyn Doyley, Franklin College

The Young Voices project began two years ago after a generous gift from Driftnet Poets. When the group folded in 2015, it was decided to invest remaining funds in an initiative for young writers, enabling a series of workshops and events designed to instil confidence and experience in performance. From small beginnings, the writers have grown in stature. *In Case of an Emergency* is testament to their talent.

With Arts Council support, La Luna Press has set up workshops and provided one-to-one editorial input for each Young Voices participant. Working with professional writers and editors, these fledgling poets and prose writers have experienced editorial scrutiny and received guidance as to how they might develop their writing. Giving writers a unique and valuable opportunity to showcase their work in a published volume, this anthology is the culmination of that process.

Featuring art from young freelance artist, Sophie Ashton, and photographic work from Franklin student B.D., alongside original creative writing, the anthology displays the energy and concerns of its contributors. The voices are, at times, troubled; this is raw, nascent talent that reflects the complex and challenging world faced by this generation. There are brave, unflinching and powerful moments, and freely expressed thoughts and feelings.

La Luna is committed to supporting emerging writers and artists. This debut collection reflects the desire of the editors to encourage and nurture talented young people as they explore their ideas and take their first steps into the worlds of professional writing, publishing and performance.

Josie Moon and Nick Triplow

BAILEY HODSON

In case of an emergency

In case of an emergency,
please fold into yourself,
pack your softest blanket,
remove the broken screams
from your throat. Slot them into
your back pocket alongside
the bad nights you sail
as though you are the captain
of a ghost ship.
Slip into an envelope
sealed with safety pins
before shipping yourself
to the last place
you could truly call home.

Dark Summer

Let's take a moment.
Lilly freckles hill top.
Cracked fruits,
Sticky juices on your fingers.

Running, running until you can't stop.

Sweet taste on your chapped lips,
Hands, hips.

Distant shouts,
Daisies, dandelions.
His teeth against your pulse.

Faceless Gods,
He makes you *hungry.*
Shoulder blades,
Make believe games,
Nameless gods,
He makes you *beg.*

All you dream of
are skeletons with wings,
Pomegranate seeds,
Unkempt promises.

Red teeth,
Cold fingertips.
You exist in melancholy.

Voice like your mother's spring roses.
Dew drop eyes,
No voice of reason.

Golden orange skin,
Pumping heart,
Tracing where your veins begin.

Bones littering damp mud
Like a graveyard.

Angels holding guns
And expensive cigarettes.
What prayers do you
Speak when *God is not listening?*

SUNSHINE

I proposed to the sun early this morning and he replied:
*baby, you're a nectarine of a human being but I
can't rise for only you,* then he left me caught in
a cage made for wild ferrets with the stench of his
hunger.

Darling

04:56am

Darling

I know about the sadness that aches your bones, that makes your knees cave, hands curl into fists. I know about the interrupted heart beats, weak feet, every gasp of breath you pull into your lungs with the feeling of razors. I know about the thundercloud vision, tsunami thoughts that make you choke on salt water tears.

I know about the moments that moonlight became the perfect time to dance with blades, to kiss blood, taste pain. I know about the way you broke your own heart.
Darling, I know about the bad nights when my love wasn't enough and thorns slipped from your rose bud tongue, shattering on the floor. I know about the screams piled in your throat, the time that slips between your fingertips like sand.

Darling
I know about the sadness.

D.N.

Abandoned

I was a broken toy,
arguably beyond repair.
I'd forgotten it hadn't always been that way,
until you.

Buried beneath the cool new toys,
you still found me.
I often wondered why me,
it was a dream come true, almost.

I became your favourite,
in time, you became mine too.
For you, I'd have become anything,
and I did.

With my pull-string,
you got all the advice you needed.
Being your personal Sheriff Woody,
trying to save you from the villain, which you became.

You needed strength and protection,
I became a small tank for you.
I'd have chased and fought Satan himself away,
little did I know it was me you wanted gone.

I hoped you'd pick me back up,
you never did.
I tried convincing myself I didn't want you to,
but I'm a toy, face value is all you need.

All of this has taught me,
anyone can change for anybody.
It was me I needed to change for,
and I'll never be buried again.

I needed to escape,
So I became an R.C. car and did that.
I needed to vent frustration,
So I became a Stretch Armstrong and gave it hell.

I needed to cheer up,
So I became a stuffed Stitch, without a Lilo.
Christ, I just needed to change,
I became a Rubik's cube, and did that too.

Despite the repair you gave,
I was still damaged, far from perfect.
I worked the best I could for you,
that's my biggest regret.

It'd be easy to become buried again,
but I won't.
I'm at the top of the toy chest now,
and that's where I'll stay.

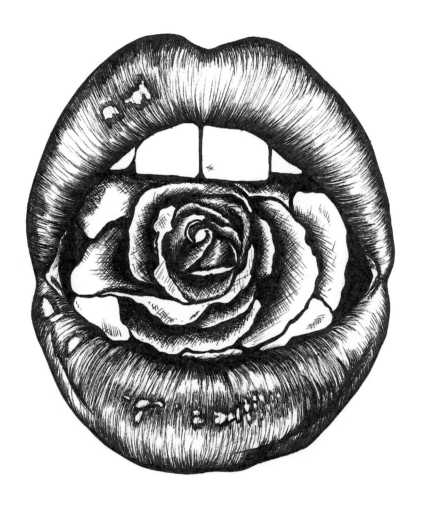

Thorns slipped from your rosebud tongue

JOANNA MAY GREEN

What we called drowning

The sheets were an ocean,
we lay beneath the waves
where our web was woven, unspoken,
a heartbeat pact
pumps synchronised, separate
through the ages, spent alone,
lonely. But the ocean could never be big enough
to untangle our nets
so we remained messy,
unmade, broken spirits
never hearts, or hands, or fingertips
because our skin moulded,
then folded around our devotion,
like a blanket.
like an ocean.

When I was a hodgeheg

When I was a hodgeheg

I didn't like tarmac,
Cities were scary.
Spiny.   It was hard to make friends   being so tiny.
Everything was awkward.
I was a target   and a threat.
And my neck became a can of beer,
and my skin became a cigarette.
Because humans are greedy,
being a hodgeheg, was no fun.
My back, a pin-board, already full.
I rolled a lot   scared my soft tissue
would betray me.
Rolling wasn't fast enough.
I wasn't   fast enough.

LISA FEBRUARY

When the doctor told my parents

It's cancer

He didn't look at me. Could barely
hold my father's eye
and muttered

I'm sorry

before escaping to his office.

I'll give you some space

Through the gaps in blinds I watched him
make himself a coffee
and take five minutes. Turn on the radio
and turn it off again. Read a few pages of a paper
and put it down again. And check his watch again.
And slouch into his recliner to stand up again.

He couldn't look at me. Could barely
look at his own reflection
or make the coffee
or listen to the radio
or read the paper
or slouch in his recliner
knowing he must deliver the same news
to five different families
on the same day.
But he does.

He takes a deep breath
Stands up straight
Fastens his buttons
Adjusts his tie.

Leo

Six years old.
Prefers blush pink,
lip-glossed barbie dolls
to choo-choo's and train tracks.
Typical.

Sympathetic side eyes
from coupled parents
put his love of plaits and ponies
to no daddy, no *boy stuff*
just mummy playing dress up.

Just mummy
who does everything.

Named after her leonine star sign,
roar notorious at bed times,
nightmares of monsters
concealed between boxes
beneath his bed.
He begs to stay in hers,
to which she agrees-
would rather him
starfish, steal her space
than sleep badly

because a good morning
grows laughter buds
that bloom and butterfly,
touching all around him
with tickles, and true smiles.

L(OVER)

```
L O V E R U P T U R E A L I S E X U A L W A Y S T O P L E S S H A D O W
S O M E T H I N G R A C E R T A I N T E D G E N T L E T E R N A L I V E
S W E A R G U E S S I N G A M E M O R Y E S T E R D A Y D R E A M E N D
L O V E R A S E R U P T R U S T O P L E A S E N D U R E A L I S E C H O
F O R G I V E I N T I M A C Y C L I C A L M A N I A L O N E N D R O W N
F A L L I N G H O S T O P E N E T R A T E R M I N A L W A Y S E C R E T
C H A O T I C Y C L I C A L C U L A T E D I O U S U A L W A Y S T U C K
O V E R U P T O M E N D E C I S I O N G O I N G R A I N E D O N T O R N
C H A N G E N U I N E V E R U P T U R E A L W A Y S T O N E N D I N G O
F O R G I V E N O M E N T R U S T O P L E A S E X P E C T O M O R R O W
P L E A S E R I O U S E D E C I D E P R E S S E N T I A L W A Y S L O W
L O V E R O D E S P A I R E S C U E N D U R A N S O M A N I A C R A S H
T R U S T O P L E A S E C R E T R E A T E N D I S T A N T H E M A N I A
S E X P E C T R A I N S I D E A D L Y I N G A M E M O R Y O U R S H I T
F O R G I V E N D U R E A L I S T E N D U R E S O L V E N O M O R E S T
E N D E S T R U C T R U T H A L F U T U R E S T R A I N E V E R U N D O
C H E A T T A C H M E N T R U S T O P L E S S O N L Y I N G O L D E N D
W E D O N T K N O W W H A T T O D O W E D O N T K N O W H A T D O
```

JOSHUA WENDEL-JONES

Why I Write...

I don't have a hard life. I have no deep seated mental disorder, no real anxiety. I get my eight hours and my parents love me. I took a puff on a cigarette once and had an asthma attack. I drink red wine on a Sunday evening to wash down a delightful tuna, pesto gnocchi. I live in a house with a name not a number and my dad owns a horse. What I'm trying to say is I don't write for the reasons that my dead idols did. I'm not clinically depressed like Plath or inveterately empty like Curtis, fuelled by sadness and despair. I guess you could say instead I am chronically bored, writing for the love of language and the adoration of the mundane.

I write with a far-fetched desire to describe a setting in such vivid detail and imagination as Frank Herbert does in Dune. To create a world which is wholly of my own creation filled to the rafters with my creatures and my vast and elaborate lore. A world to get lost in. A planet to explore.

In stark contrast I write to remark upon the everyday. People watching in meticulous detail to reveal the traits, flaws and fears of the everyman. What does the coffee he drinks tell us about him and where does he buy his groceries from? Why does she always make sure she wakes up before he does? When was the last time he contacted his parents? Does he have parents? That kind of thing.

Music influences me greatly. The stories told in songs down the years have been some of the best ever told. Jeff Mangum's lyrics with Neutral Milk Hotel are the closest anyone has come to putting my dreams into words. With ethereal characters like the King of Carrot Flowers and the Two Headed Boy *placing fingers through the notches in your spine.* And of course I don't aim to eclipse their brilliance but if I could write just one thing that came anywhere close... Yeah, that would be good. I'd be pretty happy.

ELIZABETH FRANCE

Controlled

I wish you would stop.
You are the nagging I can't escape,
Your presence surrounds my world.
It is you I must rely on to make sure I'm not late
But without you, I never would be.
You are the highest power,
Controlling without knowing.
People walk through life not noticing you
But still, are pulled by their puppeteer strings.

Cast a Spell

Each breath you take is breath in time
Each hour you spend will fly away
You're not you, not me
You're his.
Your love is his
Until he dies
And then you'll never love again.

You're under a spell.
Captured. A room without a door
A door without a room
Spinning around around around.
You can't make it. Stop.
You're under a spell.
Your spell is his spell,
Together.

This is like nothing we, have
Ever experienced before.

You're under a spell.
Together. Each movement is synced
Each breath is timed
Each hour flies away

Till one day it. Stops.
You're under a spell.
Not mine not yours. His.

Alone. Waiting to move in sync again.
Waiting to catch your breath between tears.
Waiting to bring back the time you lost spent doing,
Important things
Waiting.
Waiting for him to come back.

This is like no experience you have
Ever gone through

You're under the spell.
love.
When disaster strikes it bundles us up
in an array of
Blanketed memories. This is where,
We stay a while till reality sets in. He's gone.
He's not returning.
He didn't have enough blankets to
break his fall.
Even love.
The most powerful spell of all couldn't save him.

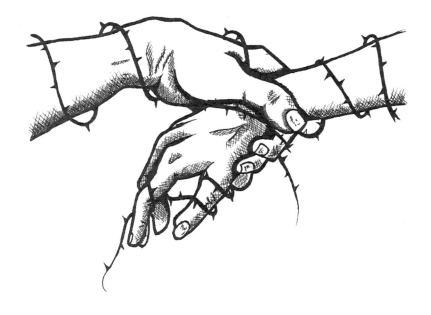

I had no reason to be ashamed

INDIA JASMINE PLUMTREE

Body hair

He wants me to shave,
He wants me hairless,
He looked me in the eye
And said
To shave is a woman's conformity
And lifted up my top,
Exposing my belly button,
Kissing the darker hairs around there,
Where I felt most insecure,

That's when I realised.
I had no reason to be ashamed.

I come from

I come from lefties' rants
Tony Blair, Gordon Brown
Equal rights, women power
I come from a time of aquamarine, fuchsia falls, sumptuous plum
Dried oil paints linger in an empty room
I come from dad I haven't seen in years
Merlot, Pinot Grigio, Prosecco
I come from loud music
Classic rock, indie, blues, jazz
Concerts, gigs, festivals
Cider to cocktails
I come from the coast
Salty sea water, seagulls screaming
I come from a single mum
Respect, manners
Please, thank you, sorry
An only child
Here I am,
Here she is,
She is made of hope, love, power, stories and words,

She is made of lonely nights
She is alive, she will live, she will love,
Every night,
Waiting, waiting, waiting.

I wonder

I wonder
When you see me
Do you think
That's the girl I touched up.

I wonder
When you blackmailed me,
If did it ever cross your mind
That it was wrong.

I wonder
When the police told me
It was because of what I was wearing,
Your parents told you the same,

I wonder
If you know that;
I'm a light bulb in a dark room,
I'm blinding, bright bold,
Magnificent
I am stellar.

People

If we weren't here
We wouldn't know about the:
Hippies, the Mississippi, the hallucinators,
The alcoholics,
The loud mums, gossipers, the gurus, the confused,
The gigglers, the wrigglers,
The drug dealers, the goths, the homeless, the hopeless, the ferocious,
The travellers, the lawyers, the destroyers,
The Indians, the Africans, the Japanese,
The clever ones, the insurers, the jurors,
The painters, the campaigners, the complainers, the claimers,
The entertainers, the mathematicians, the opticians,
The beauticians, the magicians, the feminists, the expressionists,
The interventionists, the experimentalists, the pessimists, the optimistic,
The artistic, the teachers, the preachers, the disabled,
The school kids, the millennials,
People all around the world, the people of colour.

The people
People.

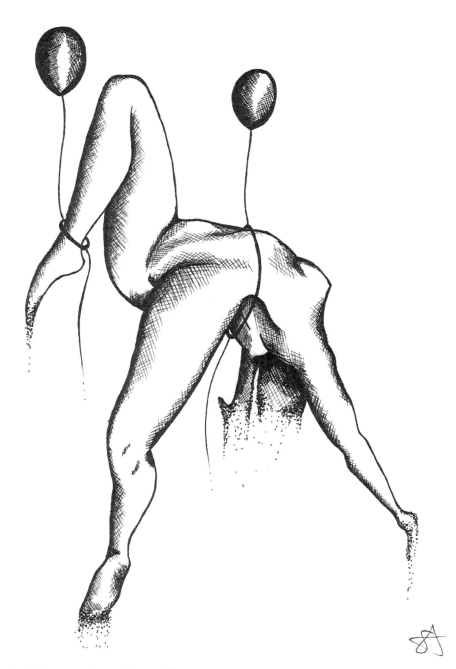

I could have transformed into anything

MATTHEW TORDOFF

The 10:35 Bus

She taps her fingers against glass,
bony fingers,
too frail for labour,
too clumsy for piano,
brittle fingers that will snap.

His voice reverberates along the bus.
Strong and proud.
The silence bludgeoned to death.
Louder than the engine,
That groans under their feet.

She breathes nihilism,
her oxygen,
the world isn't good enough for her.
It will be,
when she loses everything.

Her eyes dart around
each whisper about her
she's sure
feet tapping in tentative tempo
soon she'll never walk again.

He leans against her,
as the bus charges round corners,
together they're sweet
but will turn sour. Like
milk boiling in the sun's stare.

They all panic, engine whining,
and roaring,
and screaming as it bolts,
to hug the lamp-post,
at the end of the road.

Words

I admire your words,
you let them grow ripe,
pluck them when ready,
let them fester in silence,
I despise them.

You dismiss me as *young*,
because you can patronise me,
because you said *The Monkees*, I thought Arctic Monkeys,
because I'll never submit to your archaic ways,
you loathe me for having opinions that aren't yours.

You call me *faggot*,
because I want to get married,
because I don't want your *cure*,
because I'm *going to hell*,
you can't stand my pride.

You spit vitriol, call me *lazy*,
because numbness creeps through my bones,
because I wasn't lying,
because I tore my skin to rip depression out,
I won that fight without you.

I admired your words,
you let them grow ripe,
plucked them when ready,
let them fester in silence,
I've grown deaf to you.

A.R.

Mending

LOVE,
A wonderful word,
beneath each letter the ingredients.
Learn to understand each other
support when you can.
Voices are safer when quieter
everything is going to be fine.
Cleaning cobwebs can be tricky,
when the walls are painted with memories-
How can a woman repair a room
if she lies in the cot sucking her thumb.
See the power of forgiveness,
allow your brain to rely on ice-cream
and rom-coms.
Enjoy freedom and power of self.
After a heartbreak,
with the string and needle of self-love and care
sew yourself back together.
A patchwork doll is just as beautiful.

The Time I Was Let Loose in a City

I am terrified of going out without my parents. The shop around the corner I class as an independent trophy to add to my case, my imaginary case. At the ripe old age of 17 I realise it is time to become independent, and social – two things I am most certainly not! When the opportunity arises in the beginning of 2017 for me to go to London with college to discover the fantastic world of Shakespeare and theatre, my answer is undoubtedly yes, unless the parents say no.

After days dragging by, the day comes – 8 o'clock be at college ready to get the coach. The 4 hour coach ride. PARENTLESS! This is a big step for me, but after realising I cannot do everything strapped in a baby seat – I get on that coach and I let it leave.
After 4 hours of sitting on a coach all sensation in my lower back to my feet is gone. Achy and hormonal I just want to cross my arms and sulk.

But I can't be moody when this coach is leading me to shake hands with the streets of London as I pass Trafalgar Square – waving to the lions and Nelson's Column, and getting my friends to Snapchat and the whole passing because bad luck sat me on the wrong side of the coach, typical.

London is a truly beautiful city, such breathing diversity and loving spirits. It is hard to dislike such a place. I arrive at Covent Garden, an area busy with shops, full of makeup and shoes and price tags with a few more zeros than my unemployed salary can afford. Groups separate off in search of certain places; some in search of coffee, food, clothes – or if you're me – the Moomin Shop! That's a story for another time. I never set foot in that shop, disheartened I am despite the cute mug nestling in the shelter of my handbag.

I wish I could explain what watching a play in London is like. It makes you feel as though you hugged Shakespeare himself. The actors there, like puppets in front of you. Moving. Talking and showing you the struggle of their story. I will forever remember 'Who's Afraid of Virginia Woolf' – it left its personalised bookmark in the pages of my heart, ready for me to open it up and recall this story in the future.

Who knew a place of such culture and blooming industry could give you a hug as warm as it does.

Home.

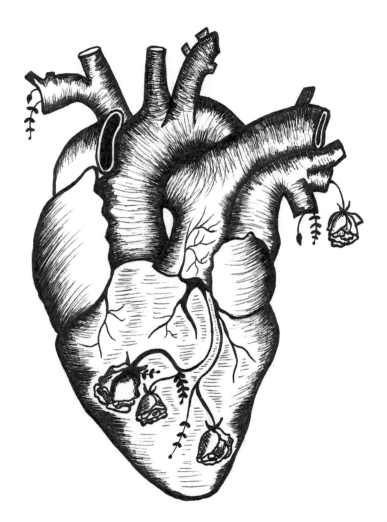

Flowers wilting on the bottom shelf of your heart

KADY ARLISS

Just Another You

Institute after institute,
I watch the same grey walls that weigh down my heart,
Their colour sucking my soul before my *appointment*
Rubbing my hands together I watch people come and go,
Dirt forms as I rub them faster.

Each tick of the clock makes my nerves twitch,
The final person leaves before they shout my name:
Anonymous Number 256.
That's all I am to these people,
A number with a story,
Not a person.

Asked the same questions,
What's happened in your life?
Do you have any idea why you're like this?
How close are you with family?
Do you have friends?
Who supports you?

Nobody. I support myself.

The same responses:
You could really benefit from this program.
We aim to help you.
You need help.
You need help.
You need help.

My heart sinks.
You need help.
I shut my eyes tight.
You need help.
I clench my fists.
You need help.
I walk out the room.
You need help.
But all we are is another *you.*

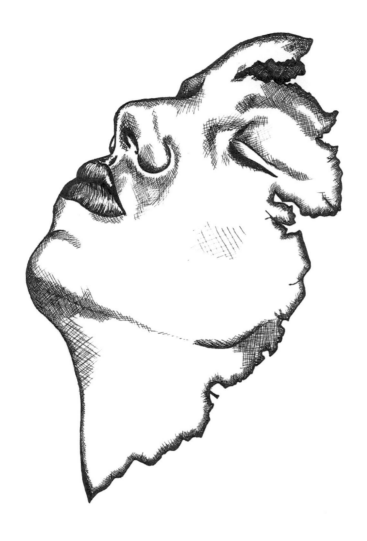

But you weren't quite sure who I was yet

ELIJAH STRATFORD

This is the Moment

This is the moment my heart bleeds.
This is the moment we sit in the back of your car, music
streaming through your speakers, and I bite a ring
onto my third finger in the shape of your name.
This is the moment my mother never promised me.
This is the moment your mouth looks like a war zone and
this is the moment I am caught in the crossfire.
This is the moment we melt.
This is the moment I tell you all the words I have kept trapped
behind my rib cage, closed tight in a Ziploc bag,
millions upon millions of butterfly wings.
This is the moment my heart bleeds.
This is the moment you say *no, not like this*
And turn away

Fuck Idioms

Play in traffic
Don't look both ways - just get to the other side.
Count your chickens, and your eggs - love them for their uncertainty.
Live in glass houses - throw rocks.
Speak louder than any action.
Bite off more than you could possibly chew. Bark up the wrong tree.
Cry over spilt milk - that cow bled white for you.
Steal your own thunder - have a taste of your own medicine.
Pull the wool over your own eyes.
Jump corners - be the best of just one world.
Be a blessing in plain sight - undisguised.
Fuck Idioms.

A Bitter Taste

What's your first name?
Pause
Think.
Do you want the one on my credit card?
Or the one that tastes
Like warm sweet tea
As I roll it around in my mouth
Whispering it to myself
In quiet moments,
Always careful no one else can hear?
Excuse me, miss!
Stop.
Inhale.
Don't lock your jaw
Too tight or they might see
The tension in your brow as you turn and respond
The way you're expected.
Are you the lady I spoke to yesterday?
No.
I am not.
I am me
I am myself
But this person
This thing is not me and why,
Why, God did you screw up when you made me?

JON GIBSON

My Eyes

My eyes are unoriginal.
Connected to my brain through my retina.

My eyes are unoriginal.
Pupils grow and shrink depending on the light.
If I don't have my eyes,
I'm blind.

My eyes are unique.
Four colours dance around my irises
In peculiar ways.

My eyes are unique.
I am blind.

My eyes see words on a page.
Sentences, paragraphs, stories.
Unoriginal.
I do not see magic or technique.
My eyes simply see words.

I do not see
Similes, metaphors, assonance, nuances.
They are
Just words.

I was taught techniques,
Hammered into my mind for years.
My eyes simply do not see.

My eyes are unoriginal.
My eyes
Are blind.

Antarctica Black

Nothingness
A black abyss
A small dome of light keeps me safe.

Cold
Snow pierces my skin
Like daggers in a storm
Clenched muscles push forward

Nothing
The wind bites my ears
Alone and frantic
A sheep in a wolf pen

Salt
Covers my tongue
An illusion of a well-seasoned meal

No time
To analyse absent smells
Only oxygen need pass my nostrils.

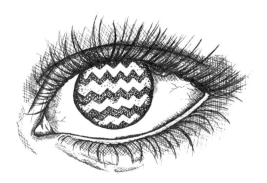

Turn off your television eyes

C.L. FRANKLIN

The Morning Star

He, the betraying son
lay without light
in the sin of pride,
in pits of fire,
where compassion died;
A monster born.

He, the demon
cast below
in the sin of wrath,
in seeking vengeance,
forsaking himself;
A devil consumed by rage.

He, the fallen
a soul sacrificed
in the sin of greed,
in bleeding for his sins,
so no more blood would be shed;
A beast with a human heart.

He, the prince
lost his way
in the sin of sloth,
in the theft of his wings,
stolen from his back;
And he lived with the scars.

He, the king
ruling an empty kingdom
in the sin of envy,
in searching for redemption,
a healer for a shattered soul;
A king searching for his queen.
She, the half-breed
losing a hopeless war
in the sin of gluttony,

in a city without hope,
taking the final chance;
Saved more than she bargained for.

He, the angel
who found a reason
in the sin of lust,
in love for a demon,
a morning star who found his nightfall;
The Light Bringer reborn.

Swimming Home

He hadn't seen the locket for thirty years.
It was dustier than Adam remembered, the silver marred with age.
Although the picture inside had yellowed, the smile that shone out
warmed his heart.

You found this in the attic?

Ethan nodded, youth sparkling in his eyes. *Along with a load of old stuff. I
saw your initials and thought you might want it back.*

Is this all there was?

The boy shrugged. *Come look if you want.*

He turned and walked up the stairs. Adam remained staring at the locket,
at the photograph inside. She'd been so young. So fragile. And the world
too cruel.

Mr Taylor? Ethan's voice floated from the grand staircase. A staircase he
had climbed many times.

Adam followed the boy, his aged bones struggling to keep up with Ethan's
ease of ascent.

My sister thinks this place is haunted. Ethan gestured to the house as he
spoke. *That old mirror up there? Says there's a ghost in it.*
Adam chuckled. *Do you believe her?*
Not in the slightest.

His companion stopped. Pulled a cord from the ceiling, letting down a trap door and rickety steps. Ethan didn't hesitate in climbing up.

Little light shone through the circular windows of the attic, the grime doing its job perfectly. Ethan led him to the back, where an array of boxes sat unopened. Labelled with his name.

Marie found these when she was exploring last night. Ethan gestured, glancing back at Mr Taylor. The boy must have seen the melancholy on his face, for he said, *I'll give you a minute.*

With that, Ethan was gone.

He knelt before the boxes, the locket still gripped in his hand.

Adam.

Jumping back, his gaze darted around, searching for the owner of the voice.

Darling, I'm over here.

He turned. Perhaps Ethan's sister was not lying about the ghost.

The mirror, like everything else, was covered in filth. Its golden rim had turned ochre. But the woman in his reflection shone bright as day.

She laughed at his incredulous expression, the sound like music after all these years. *Apparently, fate had plans for us to meet again.*

Oh, Daisy. You and your fate. Adam took a step towards his wife.
We all must have faith in something. She cocked her head. *It seems you've lost yours.*

He reached out a hand. To touch her again. To hold her.

I lost it the day I lost you.
Tears welled. She reached out. Out and through the glass. Her fingers, ethereal and white, danced in mist. He hesitated. How could any of this be real?
You don't have to be lost anymore. Daisy placed a cold hand on his cheek, clasped his hand with her own and with one last breath, pulled him into the mirror.

B.D.

What this street means to me – a photo essay

This street means a lot to me. It's where I grew up and where I've lived all my life. Living down here is not all bad: there is crime that goes on, but most days the street is quiet. Sometimes you hear arguments or shouting.

When I look, I see a quiet street in a rough area.
During the daytime a lot of people walk up and down, but at night it is usually quiet.

Compared to the street, the park is nice. Often there are children having fun and people playing sport.

Down the street, people hang around outside boarded up houses where no one lives anymore.

The street makes me cautious of what and who is around me, but you can feel that anywhere.

JAY EMERSON

Stereo Boy

His head is a stereo.
Plug him in and watch him go.

With his speaker grill mouth,
Television eyes;

He tries to stop it,
To be one of the guys.

No privacy, constant broadcast.
Daydream child picked last.

Nobody likes awkward and quiet.
He's learned to be alone;

Sink into the background,
Dress in black,
Turn off your television eyes,
Don't listen to lies.

You are amazing.
Believe that.

Psychotic dreamer

He is a god.
He killed them all.

He is lost
Within himself.

He can't comprehend
The things we do

He cannot understand
why we care.
His head is always there.
up in his clouds

He takes no notice of us
Or where he is.

He will just dream.

JOSEPH BARKER

The Southern Poverty Law Center's Little List

As some day it may happen that a fascist must be found
I've got a little list - I've got a little list
Of undesirable persons who might well be underground
And who never would be missed - who never would be missed!
There's the pernicious nuisances who call for unhinged speech
All those people who have firm backs and who might call me a leach.
All persons following norms that doctors decree at birth,
All the people who find amusement in those of wider girth.
And all of those who must insist that different races can coexist
They'd none of 'em be missed - they'd none of 'em be missed!

He's got 'em on the list - he's got 'em on the list
And they'll none of 'em be missed - they'll none of 'em be missed.

There's the straight serenader and the others of his race
And the suspected fascist - I've got him on the list!
And those who question your beliefs when you shove them in their face
They never would be missed - they never would be missed!
The idiot who debates, with enthusiastic tone
all ideologies including mine, and dismantles those of his own
And the lady from the provinces, who thinks much like a guy
And who doesn't really think, but would rather like to try.
And that singular anomaly, a rational ex-islamist
I don't think he'd be missed - I'm sure he'd not he missed!

He's got him on the list - he's got him on the list
And I don't think he'll be missed - I'm sure he'll not be missed!

And that atheistic nuisance, who just now is rather rife
The right-wing Facebook humourist - I've got him on the list!
All funny fellows, comic men, and alt-righters of private life
They'd none of 'em be missed - they'd none of 'em be missed
And populistic statesmen of an uncompromising kind
Such as – Trump, Farage, Le Pen and Corby- Oh Never-mind
And all those unimportant flyover states, you-know-who
The task of censoring them, I'd rather leave to you
But it really doesn't matter whom you put upon the list
For they'd none of 'em be missed - they'd none of 'em be missed!
You may put 'em on the list - you may put 'em on the list
And they'll none of 'em be missed - they'll none of 'em be missed!

ALEXANDER BLIGHT

Passing on alone

His watch read 12:15. Cracked, fixed to his feeble wrist.
The kettle boiled, went cold. The grandfather clock read 1:10
faithfully swinging on.
His watch read 12:15 again. The cat came to investigate.

The electric bill ran out, a buzzing meter beside
a family of ants burrowing into his mouldy bread.
His butter knife solidified. The carpet stained. His lights went out.
His watch read 12:15 again. Webs danced between porcelain dolls.

His eyes dribbled past the dry tears. Wispy hair floated
in the dust beam between the half open curtains. Sunrise.
His shirt dampened, curdled atop a soup of liquefying organs.
His watch read 12:15 again. Cracked, sliding from his skeletal wrist.

The phone didn't ring once.

Summer Holiday

An interesting question Mrs Gardener,
I did enjoy the break
the break, that is of the spine
of *The Blood King of Gamphallados Four*
no, there's more.
Had a run in
with the Empress of the Septoid Spiral,
stole her jewels in a messed up viral clip
you can find on Space You Tube Ten
if you search *Adventurer Ben*
and scroll past my older episodes
where I battle the Gorgon in Victorian England
or marry the Loch Ness Mobster,
the beloved Scottish gangster
and help a stoneager with her moody teenager
followed by that time
I chased a train on horseback
to retrieve the prospector's gold
from the runaway brake van.
But enough about me.
How was *your* holiday?

Four Dreams

Heavy breaths, thudding beats
wet, anticipating desperately as
he, below with his angelic face
opens his soul and transforms
into the morning after.
The sheets were damp.

Assembly hall, 2003
before a faceless mass.
Chilly legs, blasted memory
coach with a lion's voice.
He wet the bed.

Earthy grave, musty bonds
buried alive, a dying
torch battery, life and death
meeting in reverse.
Awoken in a cold sweat.

Ghost town
corpse littered pathways
flame eaten buildings
a titanic black mushroom
envelops the city
rescued by the 7am alarm.